"Children, who made your skin white?
Was it not God? Who made mine black?
Was it not the same God? Am I to blame,
therefore, because my skin is black?"

— SOJOURNER TRUTH

SOJOURNER TRUTH

BY LAURA SPINALE

The Child's World®

GRAPHIC DESIGN
Robert E. Bonaker / Graphic Design & Consulting Co.

PROJECT COORDINATOR
James R. Rothaus / James R. Rothaus & Associates

EDITORIAL DIRECTION
Elizabeth Sirimarco Budd

COVER PHOTO
Portrait of Sojourner Truth / Archive Photos

Library of Congress Cataloging-in-Publication Data
Spinale, Laura, 1966-
Sojourner Truth / by Laura Spinale.
p. cm.
Summary: A biography of the former slave who
dedicated her life to achieving equal rights
for women and blacks.
ISBN 1-56766-623-X (library : reinforced : alk. paper)

1. Truth, Sojourner, d. 1883 — Juvenile literature. 2. Afro-
American abolitionists — Biography — Juvenile literature. 3.
Women abolitionists — United States — Biography —
Juvenile literature. 4. Abolitionists — Biography — Juvenile
literature. 5. Social reformers — United States — Biography
— Juvenile literature.
[1. Truth, Sojourner, d. 1883. 2. Abolitionists. 3. Reformers.
4. Afro-Americans — Biography. 5. Women — Biography]
I. Title

E185.97.T8S65 1999
305.5'67 — dc21   99-20000
[B]   CIP

Contents

Equal Rights

In 1865, a 68-year-old black woman named Sojourner Truth waved down a streetcar. She was walking on the streets of Washington, D.C., and needed a ride. Sojourner had a heavy load. She was carrying supplies to a hospital that cared for *African American* soldiers. She stood six feet tall and boasted that she was "strong as any man." Still, her arms had begun to tire.

At the time, many cities refused to let blacks use public transportation. Washington, D.C., had decided to *integrate* its streetcars. That meant that all people could use them. Sojourner wanted to make sure people obeyed this new law. Some drivers still refused to pick up black people.

Sojourner tried to get a streetcar to stop. She waved her hand to get the driver's attention. He drove right past her. Finally, Sojourner stood in the middle of the street. She waved her arms fiercely. She shouted, "I want to ride! I want to ride!" A crowd gathered around her. Traffic began to slow down. The crowd finally forced one of the cars to stop. Sojourner jumped right in.

Other passengers cheered this woman's bravery. The driver became furious. He told Sojourner to get off the streetcar immediately. Sojourner refused. The conductor tried to push her off, but he could not. Sojourner had won! She rode to her destination with the rest of the passengers.

Sojourner was not so lucky a few weeks later when she tried to board a streetcar with a white friend. A passenger asked the driver if blacks were allowed on the streetcar. The driver did not answer the question. He simply grabbed Sojourner by the shoulder. Then he tried to push her off.

CORBIS

WASHINGTON, D.C., INTEGRATED ITS STREETCARS IN 1865, BUT MANY DRIVERS WOULD NOT STOP FOR BLACK PEOPLE. SOJOURNER INSISTED THAT SHE BE ALLOWED TO RIDE.

CORBIS/Peter Harholdt

SOJOURNER WAS BORN A SLAVE IN ULSTER COUNTY, NEW YORK.
SHE LIVED THERE AS A SLAVE FOR NEARLY 30 YEARS.

Sojourner's friend tried to help her. The driver became angry. He shoved Sojourner so hard that her shoulder was badly hurt. Sojourner knew that something had to be done. She would not accept such treatment. She had the driver arrested. He went to *trial* for assault and battery. In the end, he lost not only the trial, but also his job.

A strange thing happened during the driver's trial. Streetcar conductors began to allow black people aboard. Sojourner said the streetcars looked like "salt and pepper." She knew her actions had made a difference.

This was not the first time Sojourner Truth stood up for her rights — and the rights of other African Americans. This courageous woman had been fighting for equality for many years.

Sojourner was born a *slave* in the small village of Hurley, New York. At that time, her name was Isabella. After nearly 30 years of slavery, Isabella gained her freedom.

Years later, Isabella decided to travel the country and speak out against slavery. She took only the clothes on her back, 25 cents, and a new name: Sojourner Truth. A "sojourner" is someone who travels. Sojourner wanted to travel, and she wanted to tell the truth. This is Sojourner's truth: All people, regardless of their color or their gender, deserve equal rights.

In 1843, Sojourner Truth began to travel the nation, telling Americans about freedom and equality.

Schomburg Center for Research in Black Culture

A Life in Captivity

Most Americans know that slavery existed in their country for many years. They have learned that African Americans were forced to work for others without pay. Slaves were often treated cruelly. Their *masters* beat them if they made even small mistakes. They worked many hours and received no pay in return. Their lives were extremely difficult.

People usually imagine slaves working in the fields of huge *plantations* in the southern United States. However, slavery existed in the North as well. At one time, states such as New York, New Jersey, and Pennsylvania permitted slavery, too.

Isabella Bomefree was born in New York in about 1797. She never knew the exact year of her birth. Most slave owners never kept records about the births or deaths of their slaves.

Isabella's parents, James and Betsey, were both slaves. They were owned by the Hardenbergh family. The Hardenberghs were Dutch. Isabella spoke Dutch before she learned a word of English. She called her mother *Mau Mau*, the Dutch word for "mamma." The master gave James the last name Bomefree, the Dutch word for "tree." As a young man, James was tall and straight, just like a tree.

The Hardenberghs were said to treat their slaves fairly well. Still, Isabella and her family did not have an easy life. They lived in a small, underground cellar. It had only one small window. Even during the day, the room was almost completely dark. The family slept on wooden boards placed on the cold, damp floor. Water dripped through cracks in the wall when it rained. Sometimes, the floor turned into a big pool of mud.

MOST AMERICAN SLAVES LIVED IN THE SOUTH ON LARGE
PLANTATIONS, SUCH AS THE ONE PICTURED HERE. STILL,
THERE WERE THOUSANDS OF AFRICAN AMERICAN SLAVES
IN THE NORTHERN STATES WHEN ISABELLA WAS A CHILD.

CORBIS/Bettmann

A MOTHER AND CHILD ARE SEPARATED AT A SLAVE AUCTION.
BETSEY BOMEFREE KNEW HOW TERRIBLE IT WAS TO LOSE
HER FAMILY. AT LEAST 10 OF HER CHILDREN WERE TAKEN
FROM HER AND SOLD TO OTHER SLAVE OWNERS.

Betsey and James had about 12 children. Isabella was never really sure how many brothers and sisters she had. She never even knew most of them. Mr. Hardenbergh sold her brothers and sisters to other families before Isabella was born. Isabella knew only her little brother, Peter.

Betsey missed her other children very much. She used to sit outside with Isabella and Peter at night. She told them to look at the stars. She said that all their brothers and sisters lived under those stars, too. Betsey described all the other children to them.

Once Betsey told Isabella a terrible story about one of her brothers. His name was Michael. On a snowy day, two men arrived at the farm on a horse-drawn sled. The driver told Michael he could play on the sled. Michael was excited. He quickly climbed aboard. Then the other man came out of the farmhouse carrying a box. Inside was Michael's sister, Nancy. She was screaming so loud that Michael became very frightened.

Michael jumped off the sled and ran to hide. The men caught him and dragged him onto the sled. Then they drove away. James and Betsey never saw either of the children again.

Betsey was a *Christian*. She taught her children to say "The Lord's Prayer." She believed that only God could help her family survive. The prayer comforted Isabella. It made her feel as though someone was watching over her. Betsey also told Isabella how important it was to obey her owners. She promised that if she were very good, she would be rewarded someday.

Unfortunately, Isabella was soon separated from her family as well. When she was about 11 years old, Mr. Hardenbergh died. His family decided to sell all of his belongings. The Neely family bought Isabella. Someone else bought Peter. James and Betsey were too old to sell. The Hardenberghs decided to set them free. They let them stay in the cold, dark cellar room.

Isabella had never heard English until she moved to the Neely house. When the family asked her to do something, she could not understand them. Even worse, Isabella's new owners were cruel to her. They believed she was disobedient or stupid because she could not understand them. Mr. Neely often beat her.

One day, Isabella learned that her mother had died. She asked for permission to visit her father. When she arrived, he was sick and very sad. She promised that one day, she would care for him. She also told James that Mr. Neely beat her. James knew that something should be done.

James asked a fisherman named Mr. Schryvers to buy Isabella. He knew that Mr. Schryvers would be a kinder master than Mr. Neely. Isabella would not suffer so much in his home. After she went to work for him, Isabella helped Mr. Schryvers fish. She also worked in his fields and gathered vegetables. She slowly learned a little bit of English.

While she was working for Mr. Schryvers, Isabella learned that her father had died. Without her parents and brother, Isabella was now all alone in the world.

After about one year, Mr. Schryvers sold Isabella to the Dumont family. Isabella had a difficult time with her new owners. Mr. Dumont occasionally beat her, although not as harshly as Mr. Neely had. Mr. Dumont recognized that Isabella was an excellent worker. In fact, he even bragged about her to other farmers. "That wench is better to me than a man," Isabella later remembered him saying.

It was true. Isabella could work long and hard. She cleaned and did laundry at night. Then the next morning, she would work in the fields. Mr. Dumont said she could do as much farm work as his best male slaves could. Unfortunately, Mrs. Dumont hated Isabella. She made her life very difficult. She even blamed Isabella for mistakes that other workers had made.

By Jacob Radcliff Mayor, and **Richard Riker**
Recorder, of the City of New-York,

It is hereby Certified, That pursuant to the statute in such case made and provided, we have this day examined _one_ certain _male_ _____ Negro Slave named _George_ _____ the property of _John Delancy_ _____

which slave _is_ about to be manumitted, and _he_ appearing to us to be under forty-five years of age, and of sufficient ability to provide _for himself_ we have granted this Certificate, this _twenty first_ day of _April_ in the year of our Lord, one thousand eight hundred and _seventeen_

Jacob Radcliff

R Riker

Register's Office Lib N° 2 of Manumissions page 62
N J Slocum Register

A RECEIPT FOR THE PURCHASE OF ONE MALE SLAVE,
SOLD ON MARCH 24, 1817, IN NEW YORK.

CORBIS

A WOMAN BEATS A YOUNG SLAVE GIRL.
ISABELLA REMEMBERED THAT MRS.
DUMONT WAS PARTICULARLY CRUEL TO
HER. SHE KNEW THAT IT WAS NOT ONLY
MEN WHO TREATED SLAVES POORLY.

How did Isabella feel about the way the Dumont family treated her? It wasn't easy, but she accepted her life as a slave. She still believed that if she was very good, she might be rewarded one day. She was proud to be a hard worker. She knew she was an obedient slave.

Finally, she met a handsome young slave named Robert. Robert lived on a nearby farm. It seemed as though Robert might be the reward she had prayed for. Robert came to visit Isabella whenever he could. The two even made secret plans to marry.

Then Robert's master found out. He became angry and told Robert to stop seeing Isabella. He wanted Robert to marry one of his own slaves. Even so, Robert continued to see Isabella in secret.

Robert's owner set up a trap. He made another slave tell Robert that Isabella was sick. Robert stopped working immediately and ran to see her. His master was waiting in the bushes.

When Robert ran by, he caught him. He beat him brutally. Robert finally agreed to marry one of the master's slaves. Isabella never saw him again.

Isabella agreed to marry one of Dumont's slaves named Thomas. She did not love him, but Isabella had to obey her master. Her first child was born in 1815. She and Thomas had several more children together. Isabella taught all of them to be obedient and honest, just as Betsey had taught her. For many years, Isabella continued to work hard for the Dumont family.

In 1824, the state of New York made an announcement. It had passed a law: All slaves born before 1799 were to be freed on July 4, 1827. All slaves in the state would be free at the end of 20 years. No one knew when Isabella had been born. Still, John Dumont agreed to set her free in 1827. He even agreed to free her a whole year earlier if she worked especially hard.

Isabella had been patient and good. Now she would be rewarded. She began to dream of "Freedom Day."

Freedom Found

Isabella tried to do everything the Dumont family asked of her. She worked as hard as she could so she could be free. In 1825, she cut her hand as she worked in the fields. It was a serious injury. For many months, she could not work as hard as she did before. She still did her very best.

A year later, she asked John Dumont to set her free. He refused. Dumont said that Isabella owed him another year of her time. After all, she had not worked very much while her hand was injured.

At the end of that year, Dumont claimed that she still hadn't worked enough for him. He intended to keep her for another year. Isabella grew tired of Dumont's broken promises. She was angry. The State of New York had declared Isabella to be free, but she was still working as a slave.

Isabella decided to escape, but she knew she couldn't leave during the day. Dumont would quickly notice that she was gone. Then he would track her down. She would have better luck at night, but she was too afraid. Isabella remembered the prayers her mother had taught her. She prayed to God for help. She asked how she might escape from Dumont.

Isabella continued to pray for guidance. One day, she experienced what she thought was a vision of God. She believed that God had spoken to her. He told her to leave the Dumont household an hour before dawn. At that time, the sky was still dark enough for her to hide, but it would not be dark enough to frighten her.

CORBIS/Bettmann

SLAVES OFTEN FOUND COMFORT IN THEIR FAITH.
ISABELLA'S MOTHER HAD TAUGHT HER TO PRAY
WHEN SHE WAS A CHILD. AS SHE GREW OLDER,
IT BECAME AN IMPORTANT PART OF HER LIFE.

CORBIS/Bettmann

MANY FORMER SLAVES FOUND WORK AS HOUSEHOLD SERVANTS. ISABELLA BECAME A SEAMSTRESS AND THEN A MAID AFTER SHE LEFT THE DUMONTS. SHE DID NOT MIND WORKING HARD, AND SHE WAS VERY HAPPY TO FINALLY BE PAID FOR HER WORK.

Isabella did not need any more encouragement. She escaped just before the light of day. She took her youngest child, Sophie, with her. Then she realized her difficult situation. She was a runaway slave. She had no money or food. Sophie was still a baby and needed care. Isabella had no idea where to go. She fell to her knees and prayed. "Where do I go?" she asked.

Isabella believed that God appeared to her again. He led her to the home of the Van Wageners, a white *Quaker* family. Quakers belonged to a faith that believed all people were equals. They fought against slavery and often helped runaway slaves.

The Van Wageners were kind to Isabella. They gave her a room to sleep in. She even had her own bed. All her life, Isabella had been told that blacks were inferior to whites. Sometimes, she even believed it herself. Isabella could not believe that she was allowed to sleep in a bed. To her, that was something only white people were allowed to do. At first, Isabella decided to sleep underneath it instead.

Soon, the Dumonts learned where Isabella was. They tried to force Isabella to come back . The Van Wageners finally offered to pay Mr. Dumont for both Isabella and Sophie. Mr. Dumont agreed. He knew that Isabella would never return to his farm willingly.

Now truly free, Isabella began to gain self-respect. She found jobs as a seamstress and then as a maid. For the first time, people paid her for the work she did. The next year, she gave up the last name of Bomefree. Her first master had given it to her. Now that she was free, she wanted no part of that life. She took the last name of the kind family who took her in. Now she was known as Isabella Van Wagener.

The New York law did not free all the state's slaves at once. The younger slaves had to remain with their masters until they reached their 20s. Isabella had several children. Every one of them except Sophie still belonged to Dumont. Isabella had left them behind to win her own freedom. Sometimes the Dumonts let her visit the children, but she still missed them.

One day, Isabella learned that her son, Peter, was gone. The Dumonts had given him to a relative in the South named Mr. Solomon Gedney. Isabella was furious. She knew that the Dumonts had broken the law. Slaves could not be sent to the South. They had to stay in the North until they were set free. If Peter were forced to stay in the South, he would be a slave forever. Isabella could not bear this. She decided to face the Dumonts.

Mr. Dumont said he had not known that Gedney would take Peter to the South. He even felt sorry for Isabella. But Mrs. Dumont laughed at her former slave. She thought it was foolish to be so upset about a black child. To her, Peter was no different than any other property. Why on earth was Isabella so angry? Isabella grew angry and said, "I'll have my child again!"

Isabella's friends urged her to get help from a *lawyer*. They knew she could take her case to trial. Unfortunately, it would be expensive. Isabella met with a lawyer. He said he would charge $5 to help her, and that was a lot of money at the time. Isabella's Quaker friends gave her the money. With the lawyer's help, Gedney was ordered to bring Peter back to New York. Gedney and Isabella would face each other in court.

No one believed that a poor black woman — a former slave — could win a case against a rich white family. Then the lawyer told Peter's story before a judge. He told the judge how badly Gedney treated Peter. He had beaten him horribly. Peter's back was covered with scars. It hurt Isabella to see them. Even worse, Peter pretended not to recognize Isabella. He said she was not his mother. He pleaded with the judge to let him stay with his master.

The judge saw that Peter was very frightened. He realized that Gedney had threatened the poor boy. Gedney had told Peter to say that Isabella was not his mother. If he did not, Gedney would have beaten him again — this time even more severely. The judge decided Gedney could not take Peter. Isabella won her case!

CORBIS

A GROUP OF QUAKERS AT A RELIGIOUS GATHERING. QUAKERS BELONG
TO A FAITH THAT BELIEVES ALL HUMAN BEINGS ARE EQUAL. IN THE
PAST, THEY OFTEN HELPED SLAVES ESCAPE TO FREEDOM.

Isabella's belief in God continued to grow during her fight to help Peter. She believed that God was responsible for her success. Isabella decided to study religion further. She also decided to go to New York City. She knew she could find a better job there. Perhaps one day, she could buy a small house where all her children could live.

In 1828, Isabella and Peter boarded a ship. They sailed down the Hudson River to New York City. Sadly, she had to leave young Sophie with her other children. It would be too difficult to work long hours with such a small child. Isabella found well-paying jobs working as a maid. Peter went to a *trade school*. He hoped to become a sailor. Isabella began to search for a church to join.

Isabella learned that many churches did not allow blacks to attend their services. Others made them sit in separate rooms. Finally, she joined the Zion African Church, a church for African Americans.

In 1832, she joined a religious community led by a man named Robert Matthews. He called himself the "Prophet Matthias." He had long, dark hair. He wore a beard and a mustache. He even wore long, flowing robes. He matched Isabella's idea of what God must look like. In fact, the first time she met him, she fell to her knees. She believed she had met God.

Isabella lived with Matthias and his followers until 1834. Unfortunately, the members of the community were not all good people. She decided to leave the group. Isabella was disappointed, but she did not lose her faith. She believed that God would help her find the right path.

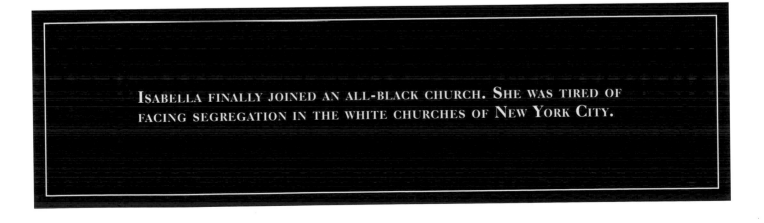

ISABELLA FINALLY JOINED AN ALL-BLACK CHURCH. SHE WAS TIRED OF FACING SEGREGATION IN THE WHITE CHURCHES OF NEW YORK CITY.

On the Road

In New York City, Isabella worked as a maid for several years. She still hoped to save enough money to buy a home to share with her children. Unfortunately, some of them had already left the state of New York. Peter had been getting into trouble, too. He accepted a job on a ship in 1841. Isabella never heard from him again.

In 1843, Isabella believed that God appeared to her again. This time, he told her to deliver his message across the land. He wanted her to tell everyone in America about the evils of slavery.

Isabella gathered her few possessions. She left the city with just 25 cents. She wanted to change her name yet again. She still carried the first name given to her by a slave master. How could she tell people about equality with such a name? She asked God to give her a new name. She began to call herself Sojourner Truth.

Soon, Sojourner was traveling from town to town, passing on the word of her God. Farmers in their fields stopped to listen to her speak. Townspeople began to recognize her. Sojourner also talked at different religious *revivals*. Large groups of people gathered at these meetings to worship with others. Sometimes they met outdoors in a tent. Sometimes they met in churches.

Sojourner spoke throughout the northern states. She went as far west as Indiana preaching her message of equality and faith. Many people respected her ideas. They invited her to stay in their homes. In return, Sojourner offered to wash their clothes or clean their homes.

CORBIS/Bettmann

IN THE 1840s, ISABELLA BEGAN TO SPREAD THE WORD OF HER GOD TO PEOPLE AROUND THE COUNTRY.

SOJOURNER BELIEVED HER NAME WAS PERFECT FOR SOMEONE THAT GOD HAD ASKED TO "TRAVEL UP AND DOWN THE LAND, SHOWING THE PEOPLE THEIR SINS."

Sojourner Truth always captured the attention of her audience. She stood six feet tall and wore a white turban on her head. She carried herself with great pride. She had large muscles from years of hard work. She was so tall and strong that some people even thought she was a man! At the time, many people did not believe a woman could be so intelligent and powerful.

It was not just Sojourner's appearance that struck people. Her thoughts and ideas impressed many who listened. Like most former slaves, Sojourner had never been taught to read or write. She was *illiterate*. Even without schooling, she was an intelligent woman. Listeners found truth in her argument against slavery. Her honesty impressed them.

In 1850, Sojourner met some *suffragists* for the first time. In those days, women in the United States did not have the same rights as men. They were considered second-class citizens — much as African Americans were. American women were not allowed to vote. The suffragists hoped to change this.

Sojourner soon joined the women's rights movement. She believed every American deserved the same privileges. Things were not always easy for her, though. Some *abolitionists* refused to let her join them because she was a woman. Some suffragists refused her because she was black. Sojourner kept fighting, whatever people thought of her.

Sojourner gave one of her most famous speeches in 1852. She was attending the Second National Women's Suffrage Convention. Some people did not want her to speak to the audience. Perhaps they thought her opinions were too strong. Perhaps they did not like the color of her skin. Not everyone wanted to see her walk onto the stage.

No one knows the exact words Sojourner spoke at the convention. She could not write her speech down on paper. Even so, one thing is for sure — people at the convention were moved by Sojourner's pleas. Some even ran home to write down her words from memory.

In 1857, Sojourner decided to settle in the town of Battle Creek, Michigan. Many abolitionists lived there. She joined a religious group. Soon, she had several new friends. At 60 years old, Sojourner wanted a place to call home. Later, some of her children moved to Battle Creek to be close to her.

Of course, Sojourner did not stop traveling. The country was in the midst of a difficult time. Abolitionists were speaking out against slavery more firmly than ever. The South still had no intention of losing the free labor that slavery provided.

In 1861, the *American Civil War* broke out. Several southern states formed their own country. They called it the Confederate States of America. One reason the South went to war was to keep the right to own slaves.

In January 1863, President Abraham Lincoln signed the *Emancipation Proclamation.* This document freed all the slaves living in the Confederate States. But the southerners did not consider themselves to be part of the United States. The laws President Lincoln passed didn't mean a thing to them. Millions of slaves continued to work in fields and factories, just as they always had.

Sojourner continued to preach throughout the war. More and more people came to hear her speak. President Lincoln invited Sojourner to the White House. Even the president respected her views. After her visit, she said, "I am proud to say that I never was treated with more kindness and cordiality than I was by the great and good man Abraham Lincoln."

The war between the northern and southern states lasted until 1865. More than 600,000 soldiers were killed. When the South finally surrendered, four million slaves were freed. Sojourner saw her dream of freedom for African Americans come true, but she understood that "freedom" and "equality" were two different things. There was still much work to be done.

Library of Congress

PRESIDENT LINCOLN INVITED SOJOURNER TO THE WHITE HOUSE IN 1864. SHE WAS GREATLY HONORED. SOJOURNER TOLD PRESIDENT LINCOLN THAT SHE HAD NEVER HEARD OF HIM BEFORE HE BECAME THE PRESIDENT. HE REPLIED, "I HAD HEARD OF YOU MANY TIMES BEFORE THAT."

CORBIS

AFRICAN AMERICAN MEN LINE UP TO VOTE IN 1868. THE 14TH
AMENDMENT GAVE BLACK MEN THE RIGHT TO VOTE, BUT WOMEN
OF ALL RACES WOULD HAVE TO WAIT MANY MORE YEARS.

After the War

In December 1865, Congress passed the 13th *Amendment*. This act formally freed all slaves in the United States. Unfortunately, it did not mean that whites treated them well. Many people continued to believe that blacks were inferior. Sojourner Truth still had work to do — both for African Americans and for women.

The government appointed Sojourner to the Federal Freedman's Bureau. This organization helped former slaves start their lives as free men and women. Sojourner helped black women learn skills to help them find jobs. In 1868, the 14th Amendment granted black men the right to vote. Sojourner knew this was a big step, but women of any color still could not vote. She continued to work with the suffragists. In 1872, she even tried to cast a vote in the presidential election. Workers blocked her entrance to the voting booth.

Sojourner also continued to preach. Some people admired her. Others hated her. Her honesty and her unusual appearance struck almost everyone she met.

Over time, Sojourner became ill. She died in Battle Creek in 1883. She was about 86 years old. Sojourner had not been afraid of death, anymore than she had feared life. She believed that God would still accompany her on her final journey.

More than 1,000 people attended the funeral of Sojourner Truth. Well-known abolitionists and suffragists spoke to the crowd. They told everyone about the remarkable woman named Sojourner Truth.

Sojourner was one of the first black women to fight for the freedom of African American slaves. She was also among the first black women to fight for women's suffrage. Her activities were not always recognized during her lifetime. Today, many people have honored her name. In 1986, the U.S. Postal Service designed a postal stamp with Sojourner's picture. In 1997, NASA launched a probe to study Mars. That probe was named *Sojourner* in honor of Sojourner Truth.

African Americans have always faced *discrimination*. The journey to freedom has not come easily or quickly. In 1865, Sojourner Truth fought for her right to ride a streetcar in Washington, D.C. In 1955, a woman named Rosa Parks faced a similar challenge. A white man wanted her seat on an Alabama bus. Mrs. Parks would not give it up. She believed she had the same rights as he did. The courage of Rosa Parks encouraged other African Americans to demand equality. Sojourner had inspired people in the same way 90 years earlier.

After the Civil War, Sojourner Truth knew that African Americans were not truly free. She had been right. Nearly a century later, things were scarcely any different. Even today, there is still a long road to travel.

Schomburg Center for Research in Black Culture

EVEN AS SHE GREW OLDER, SOJOURNER CONTINUED TO TRAVEL, TELLING PEOPLE WHAT SHE BELIEVED WAS THE TRUTH.

SOJOURNER TRUTH.

NARRATIVE

OF

SOJOURNER TRUTH,

A

NORTHERN SLAVE,

EMANCIPATED FROM BODILY SERVITUDE BY THE
STATE OF NEW YORK, IN 1828.

WITH A PORTRAIT.

"Sweet is the virgin honey, though the wild bee store it in a reed;
And bright the jewelled band that circleth an Ethiop's arm;
Pure are the grains of gold in the turbid stream of the Ganges;
And fair the living flowers that spring from the dull cold sod.
Wherefore, thou gentle student, bend thine ear to my speech,
For I also am as thou art; our hearts can commune together:
To meanest matters will I stoop, for mean is the lot of mortal;
I will rise to noblest themes, for the soul hath a heritage of glory."

NEW YORK:

PUBLISHED FOR THE AUTHOR.
1853.

IN 1850, SOJOURNER TOLD HER STORY TO A WHITE ABOLITIONIST NAMED OLIVE GILBERT. OLIVE PUBLISHED A BOOK CALLED *THE NARRATIVE OF SOJOURNER TRUTH.* TODAY, READERS ARE STILL INSPIRED BY SOJOURNER'S COURAGE AND STRENGTH.

Timeline

1797 — Isabella Bomefree is born a slave in the state of New York.

1806 — Isabella's first master, Mr. Johannes Hardenbergh, dies. John Neely buys Isabella.

1809 — Mr. Schryvers buys Isabella.

1810 — John Dumont buys Isabella.

1827 — New York frees many of the slaves living within its borders. Isabella escapes the Dumont household. She then goes to court to free her son, Peter.

1832–1833 — Isabella meets Robert Matthews, known as Prophet Matthias. She joins his religious community in New York City.

1834 — Isabella leaves the religious community of Robert Matthews.

1843 — Isabella changes her name to Sojourner Truth. She leaves New York to travel and preach.

1850 — *The Narrative of Sojourner Truth* is published.

1851 — Sojourner attends a women's rights convention in Akron, Ohio. She delivers a famous speech.

1857 — Sojourner buys a home near Battle Creek, Michigan.

1861 — The American Civil War begins.

1863 — President Abraham Lincoln signs the Emancipation Proclamation.

1864 — Sojourner meets with President Lincoln at the White House.

1865 — Washington, D.C., integrates its streetcars. Sojourner demands that drivers allow her to ride.

1872 — Sojourner attempts to vote in a presidential election. She is refused entry to the polling place in Battle Creek.

1883 — Sojourner Truth dies.

Glossary

abolitionists
(ab-o-LISH-e-nests)
Abolitionists were people who wanted to end slavery in the United States. Sojourner Truth was an abolitionist.

African American
(AF-ri-kan uh-MAYR-ih-kan)
An African American is a black American whose ancestors came from Africa. Sojourner Truth was an African American.

amendment
(uh-MEND-mint)
An amendment is a formal change to the U.S. Constitution. The 14th Amendment allowed black men the right to vote in the United States.

American Civil War
(uh-MAYR-ih-kan SIV-el WAR)
The American Civil War was fought between the northern and southern states. The war lasted for four years between 1861 and 1865.

Christian
(KRISH-chen)
A Christian is someone who believes the teachings of Jesus Christ. Sojourner Truth was a Christian.

discrimination
(dis-krim-ih-NAY-shun)
Discrimination is the unfair treatment of people simply because they are different. African Americans have suffered discrimination by whites.

Emancipation Proclamation
(ee-man-se-PAY-shun prok-le-MAY-shun)
The Emancipation Proclamation was enacted by President Lincoln in January 1863. It stated that slaves in the southern United States were free.

illiterate
(il-LIT-er-et)
If people are illiterate, they cannot read and write. Slave owners wanted their slaves to be illiterate.

integrate
(INT-uh-grayt)
If people integrate something, they allow it to be used equally by all races. In 1865, Washington, D.C., decided to integrate its streetcars.

lawyer
(LOY-er)
A lawyer is someone who goes to court for people. Sojourner Truth hired a lawyer to help her son, Peter.

Glossary

masters
(MAS-terz)
Masters were people who owned slaves. Mr. Johannes Hardenbergh was Sojourner Truth's first master.

plantations
(plan-TAY-shenz)
Plantations are large farms that grow crops. Before slavery was abolished in the United States, many plantations in the South used slaves for free labor.

Quaker
(KWAY-ker)
A Quaker is someone who belongs to the Religious Order of Friends. Quakers believe that all people are equal.

revivals
(ree-VY-vulz)
A revival is a meeting where people gather to share religious feelings. Sojourner Truth often spoke at revivals.

slave
(SLAYV)
A slave is a person who is forced to work for others without pay. Slavery became illegal in the United States when the North won the Civil War.

suffragists
(SUFF-ruh-justs)
The suffragists were women who fought for the right to vote in the United States. Women were finally allowed to vote in 1920.

trade school
(TRAYD SKOOL)
A trade school is a place where people go to learn a skill. Sojourner's son Peter, attended a trade school to become a sailor.

trial
(TRY-el)
A trial is the act of going before a judge to prove something. Sojourner Truth went to trial to prove that Solomon Gedney had broken the law.

Index

For Further Information

Books

Ferris, Jeri. *Walking the Road to Freedom.* Minneapolis, MN:
Carolrhoda Books, 1988.

McKissack, Pat. *Sojourner Truth: Ain't I a Woman?* New York:
Scholastic Paperbacks, 1994.

Web sites

The Sojourner Truth home page:
http://www.sojournertruth.org/

For more information on the Mars Pathfinder named for Sojourner
Truth:
http://emma.la.asu.edu/PATHFINDER/sojourner_stamp.html

A list of Web sites about Sojourner Truth:
http://www.iserv.net/~ckm/hsbc/sojlist.htm

To take a quiz about Sojourner and other famous African Americans:
http://www.brightmoments.com/blackhistory/fnsotrue.html